W9-BZP-112

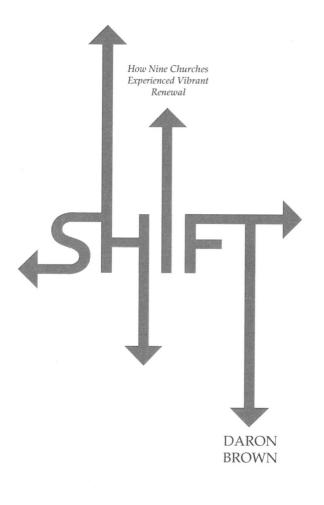

*How Nine Churches
Experienced Vibrant
Renewal*

DARON
BROWN

BEACON HILL PRESS
OF KANSAS CITY

Copyright 2012
By Daron Brown and Beacon Hill Press of Kansas City

ISBN 978-0-8341-2883-5

Printed in the
United States of America

Cover Design: J.R. Caines
Inside Design: Sharon Page

All Scripture quotations not otherwise designated are from *The Holy Bible, New International Version*® (NIV 2011®). Copyright © 1973, 1978, 1984, 2011 by Biblica, Inc.™ Used by permission. All rights reserved worldwide.

Permission to quote from the following additional copyrighted version of the Bible is acknowledged with appreciation:

The *New American Standard Bible*® (NASB®), © copyright The Lockman Foundation 1960, 1962, 1963, 1971, 1972, 1973, 1975, 1977, 1995.

Scripture quotation marked KJV is from the King James Version of the Bible.

Library of Congress Cataloging-in-Publication Data

Brown, Daron, 1975-
    Shift : how nine churches experienced vibrant renewal / Daron Brown.
        p. cm.
    Includes bibliographical references (p.   ).
    ISBN 978-0-8341-2883-5 (pbk.)
    1. Church of the Nazarene—History—21st century. 2. Church growth—Church of the Nazarene—History—21st century. 3. Church renewal—Church of the Nazarene—History—21st century. I. Title.
    BX8699.N33B76 2012
    287.9'90973—dc23
                                                                    2012024982

10 9 8 7 6 5 4 3 2 1